Copyright © 2017 Elizabeth Caroline

All rights reserved. N[...] may be reproduced or distr[...] any means, or stored in a [...] em, without the prior writt[...] 10r, except where permitted

Legal & Disclaimer

The information contained in this book is not designed to replace or take the place of any form of medication or professional medical advice. The information in this book has been provided for educational and entertainment purposes only.

The information contained in this book has been compiled from sources deemed reliable, and it is accurate to the best of the Author's knowledge. However, the Author cannot guarantee its accuracy and validity so cannot be held liable for any errors or omissions. Changes are periodically made to this book. You must consult your doctor or get professional medical advice before using any of the suggested remedies, techniques, or information in this book.

Upon using the information contained in this book, you agree to hold harmless the Author from and against any damages, costs and expenses, including any legal fees, potentially resulting from the application of any of the information provided by this guide. This disclaimer applies to any damages or injury caused by the use and application, whether directly or indirectly, of any advice or information presented, whether for breach of contract, tort, negligence, personal injury, criminal intent, or under any other cause of action.

You agree to accept all the risks of using the information presented inside this book. You need to consult a professional medical practitioner in order to ensure you are both able & healthy enough to participate in this program.

Contents

Introduction 4

Chapter 1 6
Concept of success and failure 6
Why do people fail? 6
Your results are generated by your actions 10
Your actions are generated by your thoughts 11

Chapter 2 12
Transform your life 12
3 personal habits 12
Some recommendations for reading: 13
Learn the habits of the rich 17
Errors you should avoid 20

Chapter 3 26
The 15 challenges that will boost your personal development in 15 days 26

Chapter 4 34
11 strategies to succeed in life 34

Chapter 5 38
Overcoming adversity and examples of successful people ... 38
Charlize Theron 40

Conclusion 42

Introduction

For some people, success is defined by the amount of material and financial riches they possess. But for others, it is not the case. Success is based on the achievement of personal goals of each individual. These goals are valuable to such a person; they are also predetermined, and not accidental. Success is striving to get what you want and cross the finish line. Success should not be measured only by professional or financial factors. Be generous, happy, healthy, social, have a positive family life, enjoy leisure time, for those are also success.

There is this perpetual question of why some people succeed in life and others don't. One of the most striking circumstances surrounding success is that successful people do things that the majority of the population would not do. On a closer look at things, we will find out that 99% of people do the exact same things as others. They imitate behavior and have great mental barriers that prevent them from doing different things. Of course, it is important to imitate someone. Afterall, the habits of successful people are sometimes good to imitate. On some occasions, however, copying what others do could lead to failure. So, as a point of rule, if we must be successful with our personal goals, we must make sure we do not do all what others do. Another reality that can be observed in successful people is that they have a long-term vision. The common people think in the short term. They start today and want to be successful tomorrow, but that is not possible. Before long, they give up along the way: literarily throwing in the towel. However, the truly successful ones know that success is not a gamble where you make it big by mere luck. They understand that success is achieved with patience and perseverance. They know how to wait, dedicate time, creativity, effort and intelligence. They know that success has a price and they are willing to pay it.

In this eBook, you will be directed by a step-by-step guide. You will be able to learn the habits of the rich and wealthy to be more efficient on how to succeed, better time management and good self-discipline. Every step we are going to put on this eBook will be used to transform your life even better from now on and have another future perspective to achieve success.

Enjoy!!

Chapter 1

Concept of success and failure

Success and failure are two opposite conditions that can manifest in your life. It is clear that you need to meet goals to achieve success.

Whether you will succeed or fail depends on your personal goals. By having a series of goals, both in the short term and long term, you would have been able to make it quite difficult for you even to fail.

If you are working for goals that are indispensable for your life, you simply cannot accept to fail under any circumstance. You must take your life to such a radical end where the only way out is a success. If you act that way, then you will get very far.

If you have real desire to reach a goal, you will end up getting it. Different experiences of life, especially the bad ones will make you waver in your path to success. But you must set and understand your priorities and clearly outline a detailed process to reach or achieve your life's goals.

Why do people fail?

Failure can be personal or professional in nature. It is often associated with fear as people who have failed are often scared of trying again. Sometimes, we forget some simple reasons why successful people became who they are. Below is a list of reasons that is responsible for people's failure:

- They concentrate on only the risk: their dreams are created in their heads and, instead of putting their dreams into action, they keep seeing only the risks and fail to see the success they could make. The biggest mistake you can make is not fighting or not trying at all.

- They have not found their "ingenious zone": we all have skills and passions that make us stand out. Taking our time to find out what makes us stand out would be the first step to victory.

- They do not want success enough: sometimes wanting it is not enough. You must dream of it, fight for it and think about it every day.

- They do not recover: it is obvious that people who aspire high can have big bumps. Accepting and improving ourselves (either physically or mentally) is an obligation.

- They use excuses: they are highly motivated just before they start a new venture. Later, however, they soon start dishing out excuses. There will always be something to complain about, but we must keep fighting and never give in.

- They do not help enough: the successful person knows that an outstretched hand will always get a reward. Solving other people's problems will be your best way of networking. Sharing your problems and listening to others will help you improve your goal.

- They don't surround themselves with champions: perhaps you are not motivated to fulfill your dream because you do not surround yourself with the right people. A negative influence (love, friendship or family) will keep you permanently at the door of doom.

- Listen to too many people: advice is necessary, but you have to choose wisely the opinions you will take. If you talk to too many people about your problem or project, you will end up losing your objective.

- They do not listen to the right people: we can always ask for the right advice, whether it is a coach, teacher or expert that surrounds us. But if we are not able to recognize that we need a word of advice, we probably will not receive it.

- They do not know how to define "success": it is probably the primary reason for failure. We must define success, and if possible, we must write it on sheet of paper or any other place where we can continuously glance at it. Obviously, this cannot be generalized, because the perception of success is different and varies, but knowing our real goals will be the first step to crossing that line one day, and realizing when we finally start succeeding.

It is necessary to have the courage to do things differently, to get out of the way traced by others. It is necessary to have courage so as not to be carried away by others and by circumstances. While most human beings let themselves be dragged by negative thoughts, other people do not allow that these negative thoughts determine their success. Only a few dare to go out or think outside the box. They must know that mediocrity is on the busiest highway and that they must leave that road and have the courage to travel alone.

Your results are generated by your actions

If you let yourself be contaminated with negative thoughts, your results will be negative.

And what is the origin of this problem? It is our mind. Our brain is genetically programmed to protect us, as it wants us to survive. This has been the case from the origin of time. Therefore our mind leads us to stay in our comfort zone, and this is a problem. The mind generates unconscious fears so that we do not take risks, to remain protected and not be exposed to danger. Our mind does not want us to grow as it wants to protect us. However, our spirit and heart want to improve, and they long for success. And that struggle between wanting success but not daring or taking risks to achieve it produces dissatisfaction and unhappiness. Therefore, to be successful is not easy, it requires a daily struggle against our unconscious natural tendency to remain protected.

Your actions are generated by your thoughts

Comfort is the kiss of death. Comfort is the main enemy of being successful. Developing yourself as a successful person involves taking risks and staying "uncomfortable" and training yourself to be happy while being uncomfortable. It is not possible to grow or succeed from a comfort level. There is no easy success. We need to leave our comfort zone; we must do things differently from what others do; what we have always done; what we have been taught since childhood.

You should not settle for devoting your life to working just to pay the bills. Get out of the comfort, do different things and struggle to achieve valuable and predetermined goals.

Chapter 2

Transform your life

Do you need a change in your life but you do not know where to start? Your thoughts become actions, and these become habits. The decisions you make in your day to day have shaped the person you are today.

Do you want to become your best version or stay where you are?

If you want to transform your life, keep reading this eBook, especially this chapter, and you will get good benefits. So then, let's see three personal habits of the rich that can help you succeed in life.

The fundamental key that allows you to apply these three powerful habits to your routine, and thus improve your life, is simply to enjoy the process. If you do not enjoy what you are doing, then maybe you shouldn't do it.

3 personal habits

1. - Plan your day the night before

Get up in the morning; go on automatic pilot to work, eating healthily, do your tasks and take few breaks.

Have you thought about planning your day? What if we told you that it does not require as much time as you think to lead a healthier life?

The ideal thing to do is every night; write down on a sheet the daily tasks that you must do the next day. You need to schedule ahead, but above all, commit to doing them. You must also cultivate the habit of exercise, and you don't need an hour to do that, neither do you need a special equipment. Exercise helps to keep you fresh, improve blood circulation in your head and help you to be able to accomplish your set task for the day.

2. - Read More

Do you know what you are doing right now? Yes, you reading an eBook. Read new and relevant information that are valuable to your development.

The problem comes in trying to make reading a habit. You probably already know the benefits of including it in your daily routine (how to relax, improve your concentration and learn new things), but perhaps the mistake is that you are not setting it aside as a mandatory task.

Some recommendations for reading:

- Start with something you like, maybe an article about that topic you're passionate about, or a classic literature book or a personal development topic that you find interesting.

- Look for a specific moment of the day; it could also be at night.

- Start small and dedicate only 5-10 minutes, adding another 5 each day. There is no doubt that it is easy to get hooked.

- Talk with your family or friends about what you read and share the process and the learnings.

- Read short stories or novels for children. There is a saying that stories were made to make the children sleep, and to wake up the adults. If you are trying to learn a new language, it is also advisable to speak with the natives. Some cute kids' stories you can read include the "Adventures of Huckleberry Finn," among others.

- If you are not interested in what you read, change it, remember that it is not an obligation but that you do it because you want to open your mind and grow as a person.

You will see how in a short time you awaken a fascinating curiosity that had been asleep in you since childhood.

Start also in the books and blogs of travel and personal development, but that can be a personal choice, the important thing is to make it an habit.

Enjoy your reading moment and immerse yourself in what you read.

3. - Travel often and be a tourist in your city

Despite what many people think, we live in the best moment in history. Today we can travel more than 10,000 kilometers away for very little money. The consequence is that more and more people decide to travel a lot and further.

However, in the society we live in, the vast majority decide to base their happiness on buying material goods. Did you know that science has shown that experiences make you happier than possessions?

According to the latest study by Cornell University, in the United States, living experiences gives you satisfaction before and after living them. On the other hand, the feeling of happiness of material goods is more ephemeral: it goes away as soon as you have bought them.

Traveling and more specifically traveling alone, was a turning point in the life of many successful people.

Build A Successful Mindset

Travel experiences help you in many areas:

- Get out of your comfort zone often, facing your fears and insecurities.

- Be aware of what you want to do with your time.

- To know more about yourself (a consequence of the previous ones).

- Meet incredible people and open up to other points of view.

- Expose to new ideas, new circumstances and above all, self-knowledge.

Interestingly, traveling can become a habit for you, a very healthy addiction that when you try it, you wouldn't want stop.

But, you do not need to go thousands of kilometers away either. By doing tourism in your own city or in the place where you live, you will discover places you did not even know before. In essence, you do not need a vacation for this.

Try to look around where you live, and you will see the number of things you learn. Travel as much as you can, and you will improve your life.

Learn the habits of the rich

Here are 10 habits that make people rich, that poor people ignore.

1. *They eat well*

There was once research on the habits of the rich and the poor - through interviews with real people. It was found that 70 percent of rich people eat less than 300 calories of junk food each day. By contrast, 97 percent of poor people consume more than 300 calories of junk food a day[1].

2. *They keep their thoughts only to themselves*

Only fools really disclose everything that is in their mind.

Are you a person who let all their thoughts escape? Enough. You're not making yourself attractive to people who can invest in you. It projects you as someone who is not calm or creative, in fact, you are marked as unsafe, potentially treacherous and definitely not someone who will listen and follow good counsel.

---

[1] http://www.news.com.au/lifestyle/things-rich-people-do-which-poor-people-dont/news-story/43914dba2bb89aed84f2ce59d2dc4ea9

3. Goals

Eighty percent of the rich are concentrated on meeting a unique goal, comparing to only 12 percent of the poor. The numbers of times the rich have to write their objectives are 4 times compared to the poor.

4. They stay in shape

A healthy body has a close relationship with a healthy mind. That is, we can say that one depends on the other reciprocally. The comparison rate between the rich and the poor who practice aerobic exercises are respectively 76% and 23%. And the rich do it at least 4 times a week.

5. They are organized

A person is organized when he systematically keeps things according to the meaning they have for him. For example, if you leave what does not serve you at all, nor can it be useful to you, somewhere other than the wastebasket or the dustbin, then you are a disorganized person. Poor persons are unorganized; they do not list those things that are most important to them. Do you want good advice? Use a sheet of paper. It feels good to cross things with a pencil.

6. They read

Interestingly, the rich tend to read with their children much more than poor people do. Some people climb to the top because they have used their time reading wisely. When they embark on reading a book, they do it not only to finish it, but to obtain something from it. For these people, reading textbooks at school was never merely a vehicle to pass the exams, but a way to further expand their knowledge. So, if you want to get rich and get money, then stop playing Angry Birds and take a book and read it because at least, you can learn from the rich people.

7. They have an action mentality

Ordinary people have a lottery mentality; the masses are waiting to choose the right numbers and praying for prosperity. The big guys, on the other hand, are solving problems and creating solutions.

Most are waiting for God, the government, their boss, or their spouse to do something for them. It is the level of thinking of an average person that generates this approach to life while the clock is still ticking. The rich man acts according to what they want and tries to achieve it.

8. They do not look at "Miss Janette."

We all know that watching reality shows or similar programs will turn your brain into an eggplant or possibly pumpkin puree. Either way, if you do, you are doing the number one activity that prevents anyone from becoming someone in life. 67 percent of rich people watch one hour or less of television a day - and from that number, only 6 percent watch reality shows. Yes, only 6 percent, compared to 78 percent of the poor people[2].

9. They do not bet

Only 23 percent of rich people play games of chance, compared to 52 percent of poor people. Keep in mind these statistics refer to Australians, so the number of players is probably significantly higher in a country like America.

10. They carry out their own career

You can generate prosperity and abundance in your life by changing your mentality and developing an intelligent work system. It is important that you understand and put yourself into action so that your life is a success. Start changing your limiting beliefs and switch to empowering beliefs.

Errors you should avoid

One of the main problems in any process of change is not knowing where to start. If you are one of the adventurers, pay a lot of attention because the

---

[2] https://www.entrepreneur.com/article/249269

following list can help you to prevent the main causes of those bulging failure figures.

No matter what the goals, dreams or personal changes you want to achieve in your life, the reality is that these things require commitment, focus, hard work, courage, and determination. There is no way you can achieve your goals in life without these key elements.

Although we all know that they are necessary to achieve what we set out to do, you may stop at some point along the way, start again and finally give up thinking it is too hard.

On your road to success, you must take into account these seven factors. Else, you might not be able to achieve your objective, and you will end up giving up.

That is why you should avoid these seven common mistakes to improve your chances and give 100% of you.

1. Wait for quick results

This error can have a very significant impact on your belief and motivation towards success. If you expect quick results and do not receive them, it is possible that, as time passes, you lose your confidence.

Never underestimate the power of patience when it comes to persevering and working hard towards your goals. Patience is the virtue that will keep you on your journey to success.

2. See failure as a signal to give up

Failing many times is difficult, but it does not make it impossible for you to get up and start again. You only have control of your life when you face your mistakes and overcome failure. You are the only one who has the power to choose the impact you want these failures to have in your life.

You can choose to see it as a signal (the easy option) and give up, or you can choose to get up and start over. Keep in mind these 3 important questions you should ask yourself to stay motivated towards achieving your goals:

    a) What was the reason for my failure?

    b) Why do I really want to achieve this goal?

    c) What would someone else say if he were in my place?

3. Wait to fail without preparing for the unexpected

When you are not prepared for the unexpected, and it happens, you let these events overwhelm your world to the point where you end up sinking. Preparing for the unexpected is the best way to prevent failures from affecting you when it comes to achieving your goals in life.

Follow these key steps to prepare yourself and have a plan B in case you need it:

a) Recognize when something is not in your plans.

b) Prepare an action plan where you keep these two questions in mind: how can I deal with this obstacle when the time comes? What steps can I take to overcome it?

c) Commit to continue advancing towards your goals and overcome obstacles.

4. Suffering from the daily routine

To get what you want in life you have to experiment and start doing certain things differently. This way, you can create new habits, new ideas and new behaviors that guide you on your way to success.

All these aspects are not achieved overnight. They are the result of having to repeat the same actions daily, again and again, to get closer to your goals. Successful athletes train and practice a technique for many hours, days, weeks and even months to perfect it. This may be the difference between standing out or being in the shadows.

If you are prepared to endure a bit of routine in your life, you will be able to survive the moments in which you just have to keep going and continuously repeat the same to reach your goals.

5. Do not visualize what is possible

The best way to increase the chances of achieving your goals and dreams is by imagining things from the starting point to achieve your goals.

Remember that the mind is potent and can make you achieve specific goals and make important changes in your life.

Visualization works because the mind cannot define the difference between a vision and an event that is real. This helps your brain recognize what resources you will need to achieve your goals.

6. Easily distract yourself with other thoughts

When you spend more time than necessary concentrating on the things that go wrong in your life, you do not leave space in your head to give the best of yourself to achieve your goals.

This usually results in you making excuses like "this is not the time" or "I am not willing to fail, what will they think of me?"

This moves you away from your goals. Do not accept the comforts of life for they are short term. The benefits of achieving your goals are long term.

7. *Propose yourself unrealistic goals*

When you set goals that you have never been achieved before, you cannot expect to achieve them overnight. It often happens that you focus your strength and resources solely on a goal without paying attention to how much it will cost you to achieve it.

Take action and identify obstacles that may be blocking your achievements. In this way, you will be able to overcome them one by one, and it will be more possible to reach the goal you have set for yourself.

Remember that everything depends on your desire to achieve it and the desire with which you strive. There are still more things to learn. Therefore, in the next chapter, we will see 15 challenges that will boost your personal development in 15 days.

Chapter 3

The 15 challenges that will boost your personal development in 15 days

To change your life, and enhance your personal development, you do not need to have to think beyond 15 days; this is more than enough time you need to create new routines and habits.

If you think that in order to change you have to commit yourself in the long term, surely, you will never achieve it, and you will live with the remorse of not having the courage to do it.

And therefore, your personal development will not have the growth you expect.

We all have this feeling of guilt, so to avoid feeling it here you have 15 challenges that will enhance your personal development during the next 15 days.

Do not think too much about the future, just focus on living each of these challenges day by day, and for sure, your life will change.

1. Use only words that inspire happiness

Your attitude will differentiate you from the rest. It is reflected in the words you use, and could determine your mood and willingness to achieve great things in your life, which therefore influences your personal development.

If we are to ask two people a simple question: "how are you doing?" If the first person's answer is "I am well," while the other person's answer is "I am fabulous." There is a huge difference between both. One person is just doing fine while the other radiates happiness. You certainly want to always move about with infectious happiness.

Challenge of personal development: Practice for 15 days telling yourself words that inspire happiness.

2. Try something new every day

Variety is the essence of life. Once you fall into a routine, you limit yourself to living the same thing over and over again, losing the flavor and meaning of things.

To recover that feeling of uncertainty, emotion and some fear you could start doing something new.

It does not have to be something complex, from the simplest experience like talking to a stranger, taking a new route to work or trying some different plans for the weekend could work.

3. Support a cause that is bigger than you

It is good to think about your future, ambitions, and dreams. However, from time to time, support an initiative that has nothing to do with you, that brings you no benefits and that allows you to build a better world.

Look for a crowdfunding campaign or an initiative in your community. It does not have to be an economic contribution; you can donate your work or knowledge.

4. Learn a new skill or technique

To be productive and practical, you must learn some skills that will make you reliable in life. Do not specialize 100% in a single activity and leave the rest.

Although you can specialize and be unique in your field, you still need a host of other skills like interpersonal relationship and tolerance.

Challenge of personal development: For 15 days, dedicate yourself to learning a new skill or acquiring new knowledge.

5. Teach something new to a person every day

We all have knowledge and skills that are easier for us to understand and apply. Something might be complex to a person, but you can sit them down and teach them.

This could even be an opportunity that could lead to a new source of income.

Use these 15 days to explain or teach something new to a person. Remember that your knowledge is applicable and important as long as you can share it with others.

6. Dedicate an hour of your day to do something that you are passionate about

When you do something that you are passionate about, money comes out of the equation of happiness.

One hour a day, for 15 days, dedicate yourself to doing something that you love enough that makes you forget the rest of commitments and activities. It can be a sport, the habit of reading, a religion, political activity or anything that you like a lot.

7. Treat all people kindly, even those who treat you badly

It's not about other people; it's about your stability, emotional well-being, and peace of mind.

When you kindly treat all the people who know you, including those who are not with you, it shows that you are big and special enough to give your best energy. You are giving a clear signal of your emotional intelligence.

Challenge of personal development: Practice this attitude for 15 days, and make it a habit for your whole life.

8. Concentrate on having only positive thoughts

Surely you will achieve many more things looking at the positive side of things rather than concentrating on the negative. It is not about hiding away from reality, but when you live thinking negatively and considering each of the bad possibilities, you will not achieve much.

Remember that situations are not what defines you, but how you assume them and behave before them.

9. Conscientiously, learn the lesson of every difficult moment

Due to the pain we suffer, we tend to ignore the teachings left by failures or mistakes.

I know it hurts that everyone else got an increase except us. It is also painful when we lost a client or miss on a juicy job opportunity. However, we must set aside a moment for reflection and analyze why we failed, how we can improve on our failings and move on with life.

For 15 days, write the life lesson of each difficult moment, error or failure

One of the keys to learning how to be a millionaire is doing something that you are passionate about. Engaging in a vocation leaves a "feel good" effect.

10. Enjoy your life while it is happening

It is not in our best interest to always defer some important moments in our lives. We tell ourselves that when we have more money, we will make that trip. It could also be in our professional lives. "Oh, I will resign and start my business." Unfortunately, we never get there. The perfect time to enjoy life is today that you have it, not tomorrow. No one knows tomorrow.

Challenge of personal development: Do it today, for 15 days enjoy your life while it is happening.

11. Every day get rid of something that you no longer use

We are full of things that we do not use, of things that we do not know are bothering us. During the next 15 days you will get rid of something that you no longer use; from a garment to those magazines that have accumulated dust in your room

It will be somewhat difficult at the beginning since you will say you will use it later. However, you know that it will not be so, so get rid of that. You can donate it or if it's in terrible conditions, throw it away. Make minimalism your way of life.

12. Create something totally new in the next 15 days

When was the last time you sat down to think about a new project for your life? And when you did the project, what was the result?

During the next 15 days, put your creativity to work and create something totally new.

You have many alternatives: you can create that wardrobe that you have been planning for so long; create a new way to save money; execute that trip to the beach that you have been putting off. The important thing is that you enjoy doing it; that it's something you've never done before and that you get it done in 15 days or less.

13. You will not say a single godly lie during the next month

When you lie, you have to remember what was the last thing you said so as not to make a mistake. You start with the smallest and most defenseless lies and you end up turning it into a habit that you practice on a daily basis. Take the challenge of not saying a single lie, however pious it may seem, for 15 days.

14. Set your alarm to sound 15 minutes before

Use these 15 minutes to prepare yourself calmly for the day that is just beginning. If you find it difficult, here is the key to getting up early without feeling tired.

You can use them to do some exercise, make a good breakfast with coffee, finish preparing some presentation that you have, or simply to do things more calmly.

15. Give up your 3 worst habits

What habits that are preventing you from achieving success could you leave for 15-30 days? It is important that you understand the power of habits. Do you love eating junk food in the week? Do you often lie out of fear? Do you spend your money on things that impoverish you?

Choose your 3 worst habits and suspend them for 15-30 days in a row. So it seems very difficult.

Chapter 4

11 strategies to succeed in life

Succeeding should be our primary goal in life. As human beings, and given that we have a great awareness of ourselves, we have motives, and we desire to be better; stand out and be happy.

Although in many ways we resemble animals like in the way we react to stimuli, however, unlike animals, our mind can be reprogrammed so that these stimuli impact our lives in a different way.

We all want to achieve success in all aspect of our lives. In this chapter, we will show the 11 ways that are necessary to succeed in life.

1) Relate to others effectively

This has to do a lot of knowing how to relate socially. Knowing how to relate effectively to others is a necessary skill to achieve anything. Interestingly, people with great interpersonal skills are more likely to got a better job than many other people who are disciplined but do not have much social intelligence.

2) Choose your friends well

Surround yourself with interesting people but, above all, always be optimistic and also have your own interests. On the other hand, free yourself from negative people.

3) Dedicate yourself to what you like and do what you like well

Find out what you are good at and be the best at it. By doing so, you can stand out from the crowd and be the best version of you.

4) Consistency is the key to success

In any activity of life, perseverance becomes necessary if you want to stand out from the rest of people.

5) Take care of your health

Exercise, eat and sleep well. The better you treat your body, the better you will feel and the better results you will have in any area of life. Successful people have time to prepare healthy meals and exercise at least 30 minutes a day.

Not having time to exercise or eat healthy is silly. If you have time to watch TV or check Facebook, you also have time to take care of your body.

6) Do not get discouraged with failures

Failures are an inevitable part of life. No one has not had a failure in any area of his/her life. The difference between successful people and the rest is how they face such failures. See failures as a chance to improve but do not give up, soon enough, you will rise up again and get the success you deserve.

7) Do not settle into inactivity

The bed and the sofa are the killers of life. The bed is for rest at night but not to be lying in, wandering or crying. Get up and go for a walk! Think of new directions that you can give your life, and that can help you achieve what you want.

8) Accept those things that we cannot change

There is a saying or prayer that says: "give me serenity Lord, to accept the things that I cannot change." Serenity not only to accept what I cannot change, but also to have the courage, drive, and enthusiasm to change what could be changed. Give me the wisdom that it takes to discern between what I can and what I cannot.

Do not waste your time and energy on those things that do not depend on you. Focus on those things that you can really improve.

9) Spend some time each day to motivate yourself

We all need to remember why we spend so much time in that activity in which we want to stand out. Maybe you want to get more money, fame, or recognition. Whatever the cause, you must remember why you do it and visualize in your mind the moment when you will achieve your goal.

10) Enthusiasm

This advice is related to point number 4. If you choose to do something you like, be sure to do it with enthusiasm and passion. These attitudes will lead you to success in your endeavors.

11) Focus on being productive (which is very different from being busy)

Get used to eliminate the phrase "I'm busy" from your vocabulary, say "I cannot do it because it's not a priority for me."

Everybody has 24 hours a day, but you must learn to prioritize your task.

When you get up, dedicate yourself to doing a single task that makes a difference in your life. It should be your key task. Establish a key task every day and comply with it.

Chapter 5

Overcoming adversity and examples of successful people

Before entering this chapter, let's start by telling a story. Once upon a time, there was the man who had a large yard and had many animals. But one day he decided to make a pit in the yard to get water to the animals (donkeys, horses, cows, etc.) instead of taking them to the river as he did before.

One day the owner went for a walk, and suddenly a donkey fell into the pit which still had no water. The owner did everything he could to get the donkey out of the pit, but it was all in vain. Then, the neighbors advised the owner to leave the donkey in the pit and start filling it with sand. The owner of the donkey gave up and agreed to do what they advised him.

From there they began to fill the pit with sand. But, the donkey asked himself if there was a way to save his life. Suddenly he had the idea of shaking his body and dropping each shovel of sand they were going to throw into the pit, and that's how it was. Every time he shakes the body and jumps on top of the sand that is now forming a heap. The donkey repeated the step until he appeared at the top where they could get him out. What a beautiful story!

What can you learn from that story?

You can overcome adversity or any bad moments or problems that you may be going through in your life. This could take different forms like financial difficulties, family communication, employment, illness, a separation, a setback in the profits of your business, conflicts of beliefs, etc.

Problems help your personal development and at no time should you allow adversity to become a norm. Of course, except in cases where you cannot do anything to change a given fact. But if you are completely sure that there is a way out of adversity you have to turn over every stone until the solution is found. Do not give way to complaints or pretense or expect others to solve your problems. If you show a great desire to get out of adversity, you will surely achieve it.

There is no doubt that when facing problems you will feel sad, disappointed, discouraged, etc. In those moments you have to use the rational mind and ask yourself: where is my life going if I stay with these emotions? That's where wisdom has to get you out of the hole and where you need the strength of the heart that drives you to overcome any problem no matter how hard it is. Never allow emotions to play against you, of course, you are a human being, and it is normal that at times you feel bad, but you must get up and follow the path of happiness.

There are painful situations beyond your capacity to correct, for example, the fact that the company where you worked would fold-up was something that depended on many factors beyond your personal control. But other problems such as having issues with your partner; being in a sea of debt or being very overweight were caused by your actions in the past.

Some actors and actresses have an excellent reputation in the world of cinema and to whom life is a luxury. But it was not always like that, a lot of them had a tough childhood, but they never gave up.

Charlize Theron

The beautiful Hollywood actress is still an icon of beauty at 40. Her meteoric career won her an Oscar Award for her performance in 'Monster,' and she has participated in several renowned films. Her first years were marked by fashion shows which she began at age 16, but before that, the life of the actress was not a bed of roses.

One of the events that have most marked her life is, without doubt, the murder of her father at the hands of her mother. She had witnessed this event when she was only 15 years old. He, Charles Theron, was an aggressive alcoholic who continually threatened his family and physically assaulted his wife, and her mom feared for her life, and for Charlize's life. "My mother said she was afraid he would kill us, and then I heard a series of shots, and then I heard her scream," explained Charlize. The young woman saw her father's lifeless body lying on the ground, an image that will remain in her memory for her entire life.

Fortunately, the court declared that the murder had been in self-defense and Theron's mother was acquitted of charges. The actress still has memories of what happened on June 21, 1991.

Although in her teens she wanted to be a dancer, Charlize Theron, however, ends up becoming an actress. Her presence in red carpets is always the favorite of many. This is possible because there is something dazzlingly natural about Charlize's attitude, both in the way she walks and poses and in what she says and how she says it. That attitude is the result of everything she has experienced.

Conclusion

To be successful, you cannot continue to be with people of negative vibes for long periods of time. You cannot continue to eat junk food, regardless of your spouse's or colleague's food choices. Your days should be consistent with high-quality activities.

As your vision expands you must realize that you have to make certain adjustments. You need to cut back spending all your money and time on nonsense and entertainment. You have to save more and invest more in your education and your future.

The society where we live is full of problems that need to be resolved, as we focus on solving these problems we will find new opportunities to grow and move towards new goals.

You will have to draw your own conclusions about where you are now and where you want to go. This is a personal decision, and only you will reap the results of your action. On the contrary, if you have an indifferent attitude, few will be at your side. In any case, if you insist on getting results, whether it is for you, your family, your company, your community; will always meet other people in your position and work as a team.

Finally, we would like to thank you for taking a few minutes to read this 7000+ words book and to encourage you to put into practice all the processes and guides of this book to achieve your dreams. Read a lot of the topics that interest you, imitate habits of those who have achieved, relate to those who always have a positive attitude and team up with them in their projects or your own, and do not be afraid of failure.

*-- **Elizabeth Caroline***

Printed in Great Britain
by Amazon